A Crack In The Shell

Selected short stories and poems by

Paul Eustice

©Paul Eustice 2013. All right reserved. The moral right of the author has been asserted and a copy deposited with The British Library.

Justifiedtext.co.uk August 2013

ISBN 978-0-9926088-2-8

For Sparrow

Acknowledgements

With thanks to the original publisher of the following texts:

Six Eggs in The Printer's Devil 1994 ISBN 1 85242 061 8

A father's life, in photographs, considered in Envoi

Botany Bay by Sentinel Literary Quarterly
VolVol.2 No.4, July 2009. ISSN 1753-6499

Nostos and *On the potency of cheap myosotis* in Apostrophe

Exhumation, Why Haiku? and *Is this a poem?*
Psychopoetica (Hull Uni ISSN 0968 5081)

Contents

Six Eggs

To write, to make black marks upon the white, is to discover. To discover that and to discover unto. To find out, show, disclose, perceive, facilitate perception. Today I have some words to write, record, to mould, to click together and to live in. But where to begin?

Did I ever tell you about Old Charlotte? Ninety she is, and lives two doors away. We lived mere neighbours for several years, saying 'good morning' as I passed the gate, and then I was ill. She brought me six eggs. To build me up, she said. She said she had a nephew with a similar complaint and this was accepted as an explanation. Next week she brought me six more. Large, free-range eggs in a box secured with an elastic band. It took her five minutes to negotiate the steps and passageway and soon I was in the habit of going to see her every Saturday morning. Once, I didn't go in and she came to the door when we were in bed on a Sunday morning. She hammered on the door with her stick and said "You didn't collect yer eggs so I brung 'em round." Trapped in my own burrow.

So what about this old lady? A record of her past, her conversation? Perhaps.

To avoid the enemy of a Sunday morning, the best defence is attack on a Saturday. Before lunch, that gets it out of the way. And not immediately before lunch, or the smell decreases appetite. Oh yes, she smells on occasion. She also laughs quite often and has amused me in several ways. Subtle, her bait. We established the habit of a few words over the eggs. They might not appear until we'd clocked up half an hour of conversation and if I didn't collect them they'd be delivered. Whether I wanted them or not. Sometimes there was money in the box. That was embarrassing because she had very little and I have enough, but she is obstinate. It is her obstinacy that keeps her going, digging the garden with a spade in one hand and a stick in the other, living alone and in good humour. Well, usually in good humour.

The smell is complex. I once wrote to a friend that I would carry out a chemical analysis of her aroma in the interests of science. I said I would register a claim for the rich vein of mineral deposits dormant in the folds of her neck. Was that cruel? I don't think so.

The front room of her lair, whatever uncertain purpose it serves, is infested with flies all summer and with damp musty smells all winter. The back room smells of pig's trotters in soak, burned remains on the gas stove and rotted remains in little crevices. It smells of the large tin bath full of sand, which is apparently for the cat to pee in, and of the old stove which is always surrounded with raked ashes. She keeps her dandelion wine under the table because she has forgotten the next stage of the recipe. It is next to the paraffin for the fire and a shovel, and candles, and copies of The Daily Express which she offers me from time to time. She has a gramophone with a handle and some old 78's. Last year she played me one and, as she held the table, she swayed in what was supposed to be time with the music. That was a high point in our relationship, intimacy and trust.

I don't think the cat ever does pee in the tin bath. For one thing, it's too high and exposed to view. For another, it has a large garden to do it in. But it does spend a lot of time indoors. She worries, you see, and occasionally panics. I often hear her in the garden, calling for her cat in a raucous voice that carries for miles and frightens the crows.

"Tommy Tommy Here Tommy. Quick, quick. Fish. Tommytommytommy. Fishfishfish."

I laugh when I hear that cry. If I visit her when Tommy is not responding, I have to help round him up, otherwise she troubles me with her concern for him. He bites her, sometimes, but then he has liver trouble and is excusably irritable when disturbed yet again just to put her mind at rest. She wraps the bite in a dirty old bandage and she survives. Probably immune, or perhaps the aromatic cloud around her acts as a sort of general antidote to lesser sources of infection. It is certainly strong. Once, I was in there and her friend Jessie arrived. That seemed to confuse and embarrass her and she wet herself. I had to go to a corner and retch, hoping she wouldn't notice. I'm sure she didn't.

I could dwell for hours on the physical details of her little world. The photographs of herself at 23 and of a gravestone; the religious paintings on the brown and yellow walls; her father's tools in an old wooden chest and the police whistle she wears round her neck. Her father was a chimney sweep and she wants to brush her own chimney once more before she dies. I laughed when she told me that, and she shared the joke. But she will try it nevertheless.

Am I expiating guilt? Forgive me father, tap tap tap, for I have been callous. No, I feel quite virtuous about the length and regularity of my visits, even though (because?) I

*sometimes resent them. Shall I retell her narrative? Shall
I record it unvarnished or invent around it? I am using
her without her knowledge. Or is she using me - taking
me over again in the intimacy of my own study?*

Her narrative grew piecemeal out of our
lengthening conversations. It was difficult to listen to
and impossible to repeat. She is clinically insane. At
least, she is sometimes. Other times she is shrewd and
penetrating - when she isn't overtired, or worried, and
she hasn't read the paper. The newspaper is the worst
source of confusion. She reads the headlines and
believes it is all happening around her. BABY DIES.
Is it the baby next door? Have I seen it recently and
can I reassure her that it hasn't gone? I can usually tell
the newspaper news; it sounds so unlikely for our
little group of dwellings. But I have no end of trouble
in persuading her it has nothing to do with us. Ask
not for whom the bell tolls, it was someone in
Dagenham and you haven't been there.

Most of the time I say very little. My function is to
listen, and sometimes to reassure her so I don't have
to listen to unwonted fears, which are irritating. I
prefer to listen to her tales of the past and her analysis
of the present, because there is material there for the
game of 'construct your neighbour.' I can construct
her in the image I choose from the hints she throws
out, and sometimes I think my image is near the truth.
I can't confirm this, of course, as nobody knows the
truth. Her nephew knows a little of it, but he stays
away. Anyway, her narrative begins with her
grandfather.

He was a rag-and-bone man and she used to help
him sort the rags. Piecing together the separate half-

hours with their variations on a theme, I have a narrative which proceeds from here to her late teens. At that point in the story she is working with some old ladies, pushing their bath chairs around the sea front. Enter a man, son of a wealthy farmer and father of illegitimate children beyond number.

"He was a bad'un, you know, but he couldn't 'elp it. It was in 'is nature - you can't 'elp what's in yer nature."

He wanted his wicked way with her, but he couldn't get it. I suppose that was in her nature. She had a strict Baptist upbringing which sometimes sits awkwardly with her rustic humour but has left its mark on her conversation. (She once found a frozen chicken on her doorstep, from an anonymous well-wisher. "God works in a mysterious way and 'e sent me down a chicken", was her grateful comment.) She told him (the bad'un), as she often reminds me, "I wouldn't leave those old people, not fer anything." Whatever that meant, she evidently thinks it was her refusal of a wicked, if possibly tempting offer. He told his father and his father said "Give her the money anyway". So she tells me, and the amount is elaborated from #300 to #300,000 to #300 million. With this she built a hospital and in the hospital occurs the first of her anecdotes.

A husband and wife from her church were admitted at the same time, accompanied on their arrival by her friend Jessie. The matron insisted they go to separate wards but Jessie declared, "Whom God hath joined, let no man put asunder". And so they were put in the same bed.

I think it was about this time she met the gypsy. He was hired - I forget by whom - to do her a mischief of some sort. I'm not sure what sort, but she claimed she was hit on the head with an axe in her youth and this has split her brain in two to make her as twice clever as anyone else. The cat bears the scars of this wound for her. (Her cat is as old as she is and they were both born blind, receiving their sight when she fell over and hit her head on the pavement. Perhaps all this is connected.)

The gypsy fell in love with her and so she escaped unharmed. She didn't marry him - she's a spinster - and she never did say how their love blossomed. Probably it didn't, but I suspect she was a very romantic child.

We move on from there to when she bought a farm. She also bought and built most of the town we live in, along with several other buildings, but the town has forgotten the fact, she says. She gave the farm to her cousin to run but he spent the income on high living and let it decay. There is a lot of jealousy in her family and this is also connected, on alternate Saturdays. Then she came down here, when all the roads were fields, and had her uncle and aunt to stay. She went upstairs recently to take them their tea - a tray with a dirty old cloth, two cups and saucers, cucumber sandwiches and the best sugar bowl. She got halfway up the stairs and remembered they died in 1946.

She thought it was funny.

So did I, at the time.

I still do. Many of her stories are amusing, bitter-sweet. Like the one about her nephew's wife. She had written to say she could not come to pay a long-awaited visit because she was strapped to a board on account of her

*bad back. The old lady spent many happy hours
reminding Tommy and I that the invalid was supposed to
be a faith healer, and cackling "physician heal thyself".*

But did she believe the excuse?

*I do not think so. I am too afraid of her intelligence to
be condescending. Finding herself amusing, does she find
others transparent in her moments of clarity? When her
anecdotes are probed for motive - for the membrance and
the telling of them - what is revealed of her machinations?
What kind of woman is growing old in that smelly frame?
What is the experience doing to her? (I assume, of course,
I re-construct her accurately, without undue distortion
through my own murky corners.)*

*I want to know what kind of middle age she had. In
the tattered frame are the remnants of a life, a history of
motivation. I want to know how much she understands,
controls.*

I want to know why she gave me the eggs.

There is much more to her narrative, but I don't
know how to make sense of it all. Some of it is clearly
part of her lunacy. The avowed fact, for example, that
she was born Florence Nightingale. Perhaps she
meant she was born in her time. Or perhaps it is her
way of saying how virtuous she was in building the
hospital. It's the sort of thought she might have.

She claims she was born Harry Bell. Born as him,
with him, for him, because of him? She was born the
Blue Queen. There is a sundial in the sky. There is a
Stone Man. I am the Stone Man, some Saturdays. On
other days I am merely presumed to know all about it.
She thinks I know all about everything - the names
and places of her past, the events she refers to in
passing. I understand all that, according to her, and

am obviously the sole confidant on such important matters. Or so she would have me believe.

I seem to be part of a conspiracy of hers to meet the world with a smile and then discuss it with jovial scepticism when it isn't looking. Like Jessie, for example. Jessie comes to visit her friend when her migraine allows and it isn't raining. And when she can afford the bus fare. When she has gone, to wait for a bus in the cold south-westerly, her friend tells me she is a well-meaning nuisance. Sometimes she is said to be jealous of something undefined. Maybe so.

Is her continuance of the narrative and the flow of anecdote the purpose of trapping me in there every week? Or is it a means to forge a closer bond, involving me more closely in her existence? The eggs lead to the stories, the stories lead to ... to what? A little gardening, pruning her tree a few weeks ago. This is part of our relationship, but whether part of its purpose or of its method I cannot tell. Perhaps it is just a by-product.

Why does she constantly refer to her imaginary wealth? To explain the jealousy she refers to? Or to imply, as she quite plainly stated recently, that she is able to reward those who assist her. After the eggs, the coins in the box, the legacy. It's an ugly possibility, to pass as rich in order to buy company on credit. If it were a consequence of desperate loneliness it would be natural to feel pity. If it is a measure of the way her mind has always worked, it may explain her loneliness, and may increase it. Perhaps it is a measure of what she thinks of me, and my possible motives.

That is what the whole question boils down to. Is an old lady entrapping me with her eggs and her age and her stories because she is lonely, or is she lonely because she has spent much of her life entrapping people with eggs and coins, an aura of wealth, or a smile that promised more than it meant to yield? Did she embarrass her nephew away with the legacy ploy?

How am I to judge this woman whom I have possibly created? And what am I to say about our relationship, what learn from it as I record this version? Who am I to judge? Creator, victim, friend? She will continue to spread her net until she rots beyond repair into a corner of her weedy garden and Tommy and I are left in peace. And then I shall probably reconstruct her as a fascinating character I used to know, an amiable independent old girl with a secret past and a rustic guile which enabled her to see through the outer layers of her visitors.

> *For this task I shall adopt a persona. And I shall treat it as a work of fiction. That is her legacy to me. A life which I can drain into orderly black marks, and so anaesthetise myself against the memory.*

When the sores on her legs were discovered it was decided she would have to go to hospital. She died on the second day away from home. Tommy is put down. Her chimney, unswept, is being removed as her nephew renovates his inheritance. I never wish to read these words again. Except, perhaps, to correct the spelling.

Children For Breakfast

When your father is alive, observe his will. When your father is dead observe his former actions. If, for three years you do not change from the ways of your father, you can be called a 'real son'.   – Confucius

How I ended up eating breakfast in a remote corner of China is not the point. It was only work, and you wouldn't be interested. But you might have enjoyed the parks, with tropical vegetation and ornate Buddhist temples. Most days it was wet and cold, out of season, but one Sunday it was sunny enough to bring out families in need of cheering up. They fed the large fish in the large ponds, bought melon and pineapple on sticks and lit incense in front of the main temple building. They bowed, made a wish, and made way for the next in line. Surprised by such public religious observance in what I took to be a country that discouraged religion, I assumed it was no more significant than tossing a coin into a fountain, but my eager young guide mentioned her lack of a boyfriend to give her children and joined the queue without any irony or embarrassment. Nothing is quite as simple as it seems, and it doesn't look all that simple.

Walking back from the park, through crowded pavements, where mopeds join the pedestrians on the wide zebra crossing to avoid being knocked over by lorries, I was only slightly surprised when an old man strode up to me, pointed his camera right into my face and took photographic evidence that, yes, he had seen a weird foreigner in his home town, walking, alone, when he should be in a taxi. It doesn't seem to happen very often, which is possibly why everybody was so helpful, in their way. In fact, even inside the taxis a nervous visitor might have worried. They had a metal cage built around the driver so passengers could not lean forward and cut the driver's throat for the few dirty used notes in the glove compartment. Throughout the city there are new tower blocks and five lane motorways. The airport has pretentions and the hotel retained a concierge who can speak enough of most languages to order a taxi, although they always assume you want it for the airport, so you can leave.

If you alight in the suburbs and walk off the main road, you notice how people in uniforms sit at tables drinking and smoking and you have no idea if they are soldiers, policemen or parking attendants, but in any event they are conspicuously off duty. At the end of a dark alley is an open market where you find the live chickens tightly captive beneath the trestle tables. Women in headscarves put down their cigarette and use their strong hands to strangle anything you point at so they can cut it up for your dinner. They are the market's elite. Outside, in the muddy approach, women who can't afford a trestle table just lay a sheet of plastic on the ground and put a few green vegetables on it, hoping for a sale. A motor scooter pulled past and sprayed muddy water over them. Nobody seemed to think that was anything remarkable. It's the sort of place a concierge wouldn't be seen dead. Or maybe he would. But I had the protection of being a foreigner, the only foreigner, and that makes you safe. The worst I was offered was a 'massage by a young lady', and the most interesting element of the offer was that she made it in full view of the passing uniforms, by which she was not at all disconcerted.

The hotel obviously had a few foreigners from time to time. It tried to cater for them and the buffet they carefully labelled each morning was meant to feel 'international'. A sign in English said "Cornflakes", although the bowl contained what appeared to be All-Bran. Another directed you to 'fired eggs', which had been cracked on a hotplate until they were tough enough to be piled in a pyramid, where they stayed until you eased one out with your chopsticks, and it flopped on your plate like an overdue and illegible letter from home. But real interest lay in the various steaming pots. Unfamiliar with abalone, I lifted the lid on a stew made from the largest snails I have ever seen, shell intacta. There might be a plate of warm noodles with something in them, some kind of neutral looking porridge and a pickled lotus root, washed down with a rather chemical approximation of fruit juice and a very milky coffee. It was possible, after a deep breath, to consider it an adventure. You wander about, help yourself, sit down and hope. By the time you sit down for the third time the staff have grown used to you, although you still need to present official proof of the room number to enter in their ledger – a two person job, for some reason. Friendly, helpful and quite tolerant of gaucheness and clumsiness, they kindly offered a knife and fork and were professionally non-committal when I tried to explain that would seem like cheating.

Then Americans came. There was a whole party of them, suddenly sitting at the far end of the room, turned in on themselves as if they had circled their wagons in self-defence. Usually, in such circumstances, you'd expect an exchange of pleasantries, with a mutual curiosity as to purpose and previous experience. Mildly surprised at the lack of acknowledgement, I ate quietly and tried to work out their collective poundage. It is, of course, unfair and even cruel to judge a stranger by their physical appearance. It is a matter of no moral or psychological importance that every one of them took up astounding amounts of space. I felt guilty as I tried hard not to notice the rolls of imported belly that pushed their t-shirts towards the table linen. But their presence massively overlapped mere physical boundaries. One of the tall, grey haired males tapped his knife against his glass to summon a waitress and demand, with a large pointing finger, that more coffee be brought to their table. The concept of 'buffet' had been overridden by an assumption of servitude. Coffee was supplied to their tables without comment.

While all their voices were loud, they were nonetheless dominated by a single rather fey and unctuous Chinese male who seemed to be a sort of Group Leader. His American was fluent, idiomatic and apparently in their service as he organised a trip they were all looking forward to. While they were disadvantaged by the sort of trainers and baseball caps that make everybody look conspicuously poor, he was well groomed, with a waistcoat and shiny shoes. Their purpose in coming to this backward area in a cold and rainy season was difficult to imagine, but perhaps it was a cut price package, from Phoenix to Some Lesser Temples, with a stopover in Bangkok for free coke and popcorn. Or, in this case, plates full of toast. Embarrassed by my own prejudice, but unwilling to give it up without a struggle, I left them in their isolated outpost and assumed they'd be gone by the following morning.

By the following morning they had acquired children. Swaddled in new blankets and bemused by the attention, silent infants were handed round to be fondled and worshipped, like new kittens on Christmas Day. Around the tables, podgy loving hands opened their presents, peeked inside, oohed and aahed and passed them to adoring males who admired and looked well pleased. Excitement and relief lent an almost hysterical edge to their voices. How many years had they been waiting? The suave bilingual guide confirmed details for the flight home, having presumably collected his commission. Before I had finished the second cup of coffee, they had gone.

By the time this groups of exports are old enough to ask about their mother country, and even return to visit, this city might just be as rich and powerful as their adopted state. As the overflow from the next generation lay bemused in their captivity, entrepreneurs from their native area are buying up mineral rights all over Africa, prompting strikes from the foreign miners against exploitation, while shareholders collect expensive wines and attend private schools. Their distant cousins might be toiling in factories where the punishing hours lead to suicide, or scratching the earth in a village where the residents are forcibly resettled to make way for a new dam, because progress requires efficiency. So perhaps, after all, they lay bemused in their liberation.

Their biological mothers were presumably not among the privileged market traders who had their own trestle tables and strong hands. They might have been drawn from the less successful entrepreneurs who sat in the mud, or a factory hand who couldn't afford not to work, or some farmer's daughter who – no, we don't have the right to guess that either. All you can say with certainty is that in fifteen years' time the new blankets will have been replaced with dungarees and sweatshirts, baseball caps and logos. They will have been loved, protected and spoiled. Their language will be US middlebrow and if they ever come back to have breakfast in China they will probably order toast. One can only hope they never tap their knife on their glass for more coffee, for it will almost certainly be spat in.

A father's life, in photographs, considered.

1946

On the steps of St. Pauls, boy soldiers, with their
braided chests
Thrust bantam-like with regulation pride,
Hold bugles in their white-gloved hands, bell end on
hip,
Plume-hatted, as The King descends, preoccupied.
His eyes upcast, his fingers clearly miss their cigarette.

A round-cheeked face stands out among the rest.
Eyes breaking ranks, he peers upon the Majesty.
One of us marked his hat; we biro'd in
The youth he used to be. There was no need.
The expression, our inheritance,
Is unmistakable.

1951

A Triumph
It's emblazoned on the tank.
He's perched on the saddle, between his legs
An engine almost as large as his innocent pride.
He casually poses,
Hand on knee,
A wide, unlicensed grin.
Somewhere in Hong Kong, where he made friends,
Served King, caught spru
And belched his way back to Falmouth,
To see his son.

1952

A woman's house, her mother's.
Outside, beside the open door,
He's ill at ease.
Between his knees
A two year old, with better things to do,
Attempts, restrained, to go and look
At something else.

Smile please.
You're home.

The first time he hit me, he cried.
He hadn't wanted it to be like that.
He played some rough paternal games
And made his secret plans
And did his best.

1958

Boat, rowing, family for the use of.
Sons (three) with ties (bow)
And daughters (two, with hair scragged back) in
steerage.
Arms bent, sleeves rolled, oars grasped.
Watchstrap wide and one arm has a metal band
Of the sort old barmen wore to keep their sleeves
Out of the beer (of which, of course, he strongly
disapproves).
The back records how a Red Rover ticket
Took them all to The Serpentine.
A closer look reveals the wind

Blowing up a storm behind his cheerfulness.

Some years before, he'd handed me a yacht.
Green metal hull, wood masts,
With sails and rigging - it took both hands
To hold it.
Lower it gently, he said, too often
And with so much emphasis I didn't need to think,
Just threw it at the water so it keeled over,
Smack.
In retrospect, I doubt he could afford
The yacht, or the rejection.

The curly-haired angelic one
Grew up, knocked him across the kitchen
And then took off for Australia.

1961

A family of ten near Brighton beach.
A piece of pavement near the coach which brought
them.
Shoes are polished, towels rolled, and straw hats worn
Full square on female heads (three)
The smallest buckets and attendant spades
Are clean but grasped with keen anticipation.
The beach is rocky but
'Your children are a credit.'

This is my son
Whose hair you cut too long.
I've brought him back
And I will stand and watch
Until you make him look
Respectable.

1970

Patriarch with doubling chin
In heavy-rimmed glasses
On church steps.
For out of his loins
Have eight of that tribe surrounded him
With dresses too short
And hair too long
And slouching beliefs irreverent
Towards his sober tie
And the shortie coat with fake-fur collar
Which he got from god-knows-where,
But was, as usual, second-hand.
He bugled for the king, and went Out East,
But only as a clerk.

This is my son.
He dropped out of his grammar school
And various jobs
But he travelled, you know,
And has large motorbikes,
So he's a man, despite appearances,
And I see him now and then.
My daughters tweak my nipples

And they tease me.

For twenty years, he's only in the background,
Foreshortened by perspective, edging in,
Turning and smiling gamely for the camera,
But never in the saddle,
Always outside another person's door.
And then she left.

He must have photographed his second wedding,
But I seem not to have copies.

His new wife smoked.
He drank from time to time,
And bought a boat which
(second hand) let water in
But got them both to France.

1990 and 1992

Grandad Greybeard wears a paper hat
And rolls on the floor beneath the spreading tribe
Who celebrate his retirement (early)
With streamers and an evident affection.

His grin is even broader in the final frame,
Where he poses between two men whom he
embraces
Because they leapt from their ambulance to resurrect
him

On the first occasion when his heart refused the
strain.
They were too late for the second, when it seems
He fought for breath, and cried 'what's going on?'
And then, confused, he found himself subtracted
From the bustling groups whose faces fill the album,
With his image.

His Final Words

Once posed, the question has to be addressed.
Like a beaten dog, he stared at life, confused,
"What's going on?" he asked. But perhaps he guessed.

His journey was more a muddle than a quest,
His tree of knowledge had one apple, bruised.
Once posed, the question has to be addressed.

A rounded little figure in a vest,
He'd sternly fold his arms. We'd be amused.
"What's going on?" he asked. But perhaps he guessed.

Unlike his own, our lives had all progressed
We left him there, the answer still refused.
Once posed, the question has to be addressed.

Had he been loved? That maggot in his breast
Ate into him. The silent air accused.
"What's going on?" he asked. But perhaps he guessed.

Those were his final words. His life expressed,
As he fought for breath, in lucid interludes.
Once posed, the question has to be addressed.
"What's going on?" he asked. But perhaps he guessed.

On the potency of cheap myositis

What he knew of gardening was what he knew of life,
You roll your boulder up a hill a lot, and hope.
Thus, armed with enthusiasm and a tolerant wife
Whom he sought to please, he terraced her a slope.
He didn't know the names of plants, but knew
Instinctively he'd have to chase each cat
That peed on his front lawn. They, being true
To their feline natures, smiled, crept back and shat.
He dug up a Cornish shovel-head, rusted thin
Which was put to use, and serves, new-handled, still,
Took seed from his favourite plant, watered them in
And against all odds, they grew. Then he was ill.
She was left with a shovel, symbolic, and a terraced
plot,

Which each spring chokes with cliché, forget-me-not.

Nay Madam, but I know not seemly.

Dead four years, a petty space,
and her tilthing the gardener
with his photo by the bed.
No flowers on his grave this year.

And all the aunts in hats,
with cobwebs on their gussets,
cluster round the telephone
to misinform his progeny
of sacrilege and spite.

But we, in scion, know.
How they pruned together happily
so the soil retains the seed of it
and how, in ways Horatio would still find
                              quite unthinkable,
he is here with every thrust of spring
and smiles upon her plenty
as the mud dries on his boots

Exhumation

He lived inside me like a maggot,
But as the years crawled on
I baited hooks with metaphors
And lured him to a verbal cage
Where he fattened on attention
And pupated.

And as the ink dried, slowly,
He began to change again;
Emerging through the thickening skin,
Feasting on memory, he flew away
Transformed.

After the first death, there has to be another -
The corpse will kick until the last revision.

Castle Point, Falmouth

Rocks down to the sea
You showed me with pride. Now you
Are ashes inland.

Water still rises, laps, falls,
Turning the granite to sand.

Sparkle

It's pure at the source
As we live it gets muddied,
It wears away rocks
As it flows to the sea

We were innocent once.
At our best we remain so,
But we damage each other,
As we flow to the sea

And far from the land,
In the mist of the morning,
The swell of the ocean
Unites us again

In the innocent emptiness,
Deeper than thinking,
Dark green and deadly
It brings us to peace

And a swirl of green water
Far out and unnoticed
Is all that remains
Of a couple of lives

Rocinante

So saying, he gave Rocinante the spur

I

Bite his face off. Bite.
Houyhnhnm my arse,
Tethered by cracked hooves,
With the cold bit on depressed tongue, metal taste
And sore.
He thinks he can rein my daydreams.

But they pass.

II

The aroma of unspoiled grass
Plagues me at night.
I prefer the musty safety
Of a bolted stable, old worn straw.

I know it's wrong,
But I won't change now.

III

I know it's just a windmill.
So does he.
But what else is there
On this windy plain?

Botany Bay

A poem with footnotes to satisfy the metatextuals

William Carlos Williams is a famous poet
and yesterday I had his plums in my mouth.

As he died in 1963,
this statement is open to misinterpretation.

I opened the fridge, or 'icebox', and I saw
The shine and bloom of a small bunch
Of cold red grapes in a white bowl. [1]

Without thinking,
Or, at least, without making a conscious moral choice,
I picked two out and rolled them on my tongue
Then, Keatsian to the core, I burst the grape
Against my palette and the juice spilled [2]
And I was ... transported.

You thieving sod, said a voice behind me,
I was saving those for later.

Forgive me, I panted,
I was having a metatextual moment [3] and,
Although small, they were delicious,

---

[1] *This is just to say* by William Carlos Williams

[2] Keats, *Ode to Melancholy*

[3] Metatext - 'the linguistic material which does not add propositional
information but which signals the presence of the author'- Vanda Kopple

But extremely cold.

1963 was a long time ago,
so it was a draught of vintage, [4]
in a way.

---

[4] Keats, Ode to a Nightingale

Expletives Delineated

Discussing poetry with a class of young fellows in trade.

Jack Welder, rude mekanical, tattoos flourished
on his bicep, gobbed on the parquet, shoved
a final crisp in the rough direction of his north and
                                         south
and leaned his arse against the universe to pose
                            his *a posteriori:*

Wot's the point
of poxy poetry
 when you could say it simply?
I talk English - not that bleedin
flowers-in-your-bellybutton bullshit.

Georgians to the wall, alliteration natural,
sprung rhythm and the lad shows promise.

Which, of all the scurillous asperions,
vilpendious and vitriolic phrases,
would you choose, Jack, as your favourite?
Lob me the Limehouse expletive sweetest to
your ribald ear, creative little bugger
that you are.

With furrowed brow, expecting retribution:
Festering gobshite.
Weave a Miltonic garland out of that.
And why?
Because I like the sound.
It pleasures me, Petruchio.

One thinks, the desiccated petals falling nutwards,
first of Burgess, with his *for cough* Enderby.
The Host's ' hogges toord, and various of Will's
omphallic puns. Bloom can savour sewage smells
in literary form, so his preferred expletive -
bouncy, and encapsulates post-modernist suspicion
of such literary tropes as
'encapsulates post-modernist suspicion'.

Shag-brained pillock was his second choice.

Is it possible, or wise, to tell him that when Chaucer
got pissed off with literary Romance he went
                              twinkling forth
to multiply in such a basic bum-including English
and without the which we all be (begging Pardoner)
                              poorer?
Whatever, sure the lad shows promise.
Shame to just discourage him.
But, well, coillons.

My Country Collocated
wrapped in the red white and etc.

Pillar and 'phone box famous -
Thin line, arrows, berets.
No squirrels, but some admiral (rum and barrel,
Sails in the sunset) rose (ambiguous),
Light district (breast caught handed, faced - smell
                                              herring!)
Tape, yes, coats, brick universities,
But still hot pokers, deer and carpet treatment -
Even nose and letterdays -
We're in the but we're wellb.

Gilbert, cliffs and Isle of.
Weddings still, and Snow,
Chapel, great hope, horse and knight,
Not flag and featherfaced corpuscles, no, although
Hallpaper sepulchre, washlie and elephant.
Slaves once. Devil.

True deep navy (ruled the waves once)
Prussian Ma'am, Godblesser
For the bloodstock (not a stocking)
Lamp, bells, riband, titbirds and a clear clear sky
So hoist the Peter -
Movies, yes, and beards with muckymurderbottle, yes
But pencil that.
Eyed helmets doing good job,
Chips. Hip Hip.

***

John's body, Sweet Georgia, Sir Thomas (e).
Lancelot's capable, nut, Gordon, Tom.
Medium (is anyone really there?) and
Newcastle.

Ing, the gravy poet, study, trout.
Sugar, owl, paper, rice, belt.
Bess, stone, cow (how now?),
sauce, bread and Ale.

Lincoln village Parsons:
Winterspring (eat your) Graham,
Racing, gang
And pleasant land.
Ah, sleeves delight in the woodsward fingers knight,
Finch-horn about the gillswich, eyed cheesegage.
Fly, land, door (oh what's behind?) lipped
musselhouse and peace.

Nostos

a gardener's lament

It's commonly believed that a little gentle gardening
Brings peace to those whose arteries are hardening,
Whereas, in fact, one learns to dread the spring,
And the Proustian moments petalsmell can bring.

My great maternal grandpa, Edgar Hand,
Lurks in the smell of wallflowers, which demand,
The immediate return of childhood wonder,
At gas light, pipesmoke, leather and gazunder.
His wife, the Guinness-guzzling Lydia May
Would send by steam train, annually, a spray
Of lilly-of-the-valley. Now they spread
All over my allotment, like the dead.
Bluebell and primrose summon like a knell
A Cornish wood my gran and I knew well
Whilst my father, to whom I gave my favourite rose,
Planted myosotis then turned up his toes.
When plants are said to tolerate some shade
That shouldn't mean a ghost that's just been laid.
One summer's evening, led by smells anew,
I bent to the earth and mother-in-law poked through;
Hemerocallis, rockrose, Solomon's seal,
Sea holly, miniature fir - the senses reel
When, after rain, a Canterbury Bell
Like Proserpine, pops up again from hell,
And intimations of mortality remain
When winter comes, and they all pop back again.

So, if you come to stay, don't bring a plant.
It might recall some hairy-chinned old aunt
Who, thus released, will hover like a sprite

In the smoky air and the fading autumn light.
Or worse, when you shuffle off your mortal coil
You'll take up residence among my soil.
And, wandering innocent before The Fall,
I'll catch your scent, and hear the carrion call.
Nostalgia's from the Greek. One should refrain
From nostos (a return) and algos (pain),
But a single leaf can serve to hold us fast,
Strong roots attach the present to the past.

Early one August

There was something special about that morning.
All the cats in our road,
                              and the next,
Were sitting outside, waiting for it.

They tuned their ears and glazed their eyes
in concentration.
They couldn't tell me what it was,
but they clearly knew.

I must have blinked and missed it.
By the evening they had all gone in,
and it was over.

But I shall never forget it.

Magpie

Two overdressed intruders skycrashed in,
Raucously discordant, out of scale, they
Kalashnikoved the afternoon then rose,
Ejecting parent blackbirds for a gobbet
Of warm fledgeling.

Up-market crows in white waistcoats,
With a silky flash of blue and green,
Cacophonous, they tore up lumps of moss
And strutted, Ruritanian, as they made
Their presence known.

Later, domestic in a silver birch,
They picked at twigs, and hopped around each other,
The light behind them, monochrome, clean-lined,
The whitewall tyre of the species pica,
A matching pair.

Ancestral

Ludgvan, Crowan, St. Keverne, Coverack, Falmouth;
the long and complex annals of the poor

Their bones and secrets season the stone-sharp
                                               ground
Beneath the gale-rough grass, around dead mines.
Unmarkered, mouldering through the earth around
Decaying harbours, they have left no signs
To help imagine them save what defines
This very absence - they became the place.
Their elements are native, and the sound
Of rain on hedges serves them as a grace -
Their voice is moorwind, gulls on a cold cliff face.

Except - here, look, this penscratch on a page
Where an old incumbent, subject to new demands,
Records the trifling details of the age
And in the candlelight, with tired hands,
Writes what he remembers, and partially understands,
Their births, interrings, names he hears as they
Pronounced them to him; now other ears engage
With John (a bastard) Jenfer, Catheren, who lay
Inscribed, to be new-uttered to more receptive day.

And through the labour of a long-forgotten clerk
The story half-emerges of a photograph, new-framed
And willed to a surviving son. Among the dark
Unlettered lives, perhaps a ship is named
As it carries bodies overseas - newspapers blamed
Low price for copper, clay, or fish or tin,

Or muscle power - an unnecessary hand might mark
A cross, even a signature, and gangplank in
To formal records, ending one life so another could
begin.

Like sub-atomic particles, whose existence is implied
From the traces left as they are forced apart,
We learn of them through the means by which they
tried
To separate - it takes more subtle art,
To ravel out their unity and know their heart.
They shared food, bed, clothes, village, cast of mind,
The clerks do not record what else beside
But, standing here, it is possible to find,
Buried within, the elements their passing left behind.

Shelter

Some people stomp up mountains for the T-shirt,
Wearing their satisfaction till it fades,
While most, being sensible, content themselves
With turning as the grass gives out
And mist rolls down to remind them of their place.
An unexcited sheep looks on, indifferent
To their passing, now or later, and the groups
Descend, exchanging jovial clichés with the
Sweaty late-arisers.

That leaves a third kind, having perhaps
Those louder noises echoing in our heads.
Old Testament, where height is anthelmintic,
We climb towards the spectral and opaque
And find ourselves, like Alice, getting smaller.
Snow underfoot, the cairns removed from view,
And only guesswork keeping us secure
From the precipitate.
There at the top, where the snowline meets the cloud
We stumble, shrunk, to a little metal hutch,
Thick-cabled to a pile of railway sleepers.
Outside, it's white as albatross, and howling.
Inside, it's dark, and others have left their spoor:
A pair of leather German boots in almost
New condition, a lilo (flat), some packets
Of once-edible confection and, without its covers,
damp, an old Koran.

No need to knife an Isaac, or to carve
Strict prohibitions formally on stone.

This pocket of the pointless and bizarre moves
Subtler than the Lakeland rock that loomed
So ponderously through Wordsworth's dreams.

Wind dies, snow stops, and no-one else arrives.
Down past the sheep, and its insouciant cudding,
You find yourself re-pledged to that conviction
That to seek for answers merely spoils the question,
And it makes, of course, no difference to the dead.

Nearer The Grave

for a younger woman, bewailing the disaster of her fortieth
birthday

Nearer my grave to thee, by forty years,
End games approach, no well-intentioned verse,
Arriving to sustain you through your fears,
Removes the fact of rubber sheet and hearse.
Encouraging though it is to believe false rumours,
Restrain the hope that life at last will start
To bloom at forty - so will dormant tumours,
Hiding in wait in colon, brain and heart.
Enough! Such schadenfreude comes too easy,
Give me your hand and let us drink your health,
Remarking how my liver spots make you queasy
At the way dark worms creep into us by stealth.
Vexations always pass, for they can never
Extend beyond the grave, which lasts for ever.

Border Crossing 2 a.m. 1968

Between the unmarked leaving,
And the prospect of irrelevant arrival,
Apprehension of authority
Matures into understanding.

In a wooded, dark hiatus,
Distantly, a dog barks, off the leash.
Stars, more distant, break the laws of physics,
and lead the way.

Dead Larkins

Grief and nostalgia,
Misery and strife,
Fed the writing
And buggered up your life.

And what remains?
Not love - your memory's hateful,
But a canon, some balls,
And a reader duly grateful

Why Haiku?

They say more with less,
Like a coiled spring, or a bud
Which opens when read.

(For those with logorrhoea
The Tanka contains excess.)

Structuralists have got it made

Is this a poem?
It depends in part upon
The syllable count.

And upon the mind of the
Creative reader. Thank you

One Way Traffic

You can call Steptoe Harold
But not Pinter Harry,
Though it marked a King (mark V)
With both his eyes.

Foreign Field

A stoppered pot marked
Fresh Air from Land's End, has small
Print - *Made in Taiwan*.

Can't complain - born in Falmouth
But made (sshh!) over St. Mawes.

Grampian Trilogy

Theorem in Canvas

Malevolent tents
Always collapse when you have
Three sheets to the wind.

Newtonmore

It seemed at first dull.
By nightfall it somehow had
Posed an enigma

Worlds Apart

Nervous, the rabbits
Eventually come closer,
But still seem bite-size

Pintpun for the cognoscenti

If I praise the light
That sparkles from this liquid
And pour it into
Thirty three syllables, then
I shall have overfilled a
Tankard

Kawasaki GT550

Hermetically,
It transforms base metalled roads
Into golden days.

Being Japanese, it goes
Tank-tanka in repose.

Haiku for a Japanese milkmaid

She buttered my churn
But then soured and departed
For an udder man

Loch Ericht

Morning hesitates;
Soft grey rainlight begins with
A scatter of deer

sweet and sour

Insomniac chef
Chops rhythmically and whistles
Wok around the clock

Compassion fatigue (broadsheet version)

I'm a modern, moderate, liberal-minded democrat,
And I look for the truth between any two extremes,
So when the defenceless are raped, and their
                                    homes are bombed flat
I encourage discussion - it can't be as bleak as it
                                                seems.
Revenge is destructive, a barbarous third world
                                            emotion,
There are rumours that all sides are, shall we say,
                                        less than urbane,
So we must break the cycle of violence, and man's
                                        sad devotion
To the sort of disorder from which only terrorists
                                                gain.
Yes, we'll send in some food (we have plenty) and
                                        perhaps a few toys
Which Our Readers have kindly donated and, if
                                        they're not black
And they're suitably mediagenic, a few girls and boys
Can be flown here for hospital shots (but they must
                                    go straight back).
And perhaps our example, so measured and calm and
                                            humane,
Can encourage more tolerance in the land where
                                    they'll have to remain.

Kumquat May

or My Relationship with Fruit

for JB

Conference Pears?
Bollocks to 'em

Melons?
Get out of my pub!

Granny Smith?
Shady Pines and no visits

Bananas?
They're the Republicans.

Redcurrants
The enemy within (see what I mean)

Gooseberry?
Not I. But troilism on the other hand
(or hands)

Kiwi fruits?
So Abigail's Party.

Figs?
You need counselling

Oranges?
Lodge a complaint

Cherries?
Lost 'em.

Dates?
Can't remember 'em

Nectarine?
A slaphead peach, forget it!

Grapes?
Too wrathful

Kiwi fruit
Too Habitat!

And hard green pears?
(reprise, good reader)

Omnes: Bollocks to 'em!

Instructions to my executor

1 - bonefire.

When they gather funereally, even the innocent young
Tend to notice cold winds at their back, and the ash
                                          on their tongue,
So that many emotions entangle to shape and inform
That unsettling practice of mourning the no-longer-
                                          warm.
This can be cathartic, with a healthy purgation
                                  through grieving;
Thus in death as in life, one can render a service by
                                          leaving.
But that doesn't give them a licence, however bereft,
To bury me deeply in cliché the minute I've left.
So discourage the thoughts that wear ties, and undue
                                  signs of deference,
To feeble ideas of what's proper. Refuse any reference
To deities, afterlives, judgements - I didn't repent
And will always refuse to believe in wherever I'm
                                          sent.
Choose music that isn't too credulous, cool but with
                                          swing,
Ain't Nobody Here but Us Chickens - that sort of
                                          thing;
Then hit 'em with Hopkins – Spring and Fall - I 've
always thought
Those particular rhythms embody the last resort,
Or Yeats - Wilde Swans at Coole ought to provoke
A reflective condition that turns your thoughts softly
                                          to smoke.
When the coffin rolls off through the curtain, that

                                    difficult pause
Can be filled with some old John Lee Hooker, or
                                    maybe The Doors?

2 - wake.

Suffer the children who came with the friends and
                                    related
To drink what they want then go off to get better
                                    acquainted.
Encourage the adults, and children who think they're
                                    mature,
To pass through loquacious to legless, then give them
                                    some more.
Tell some tall irresponsible stories, half-true and light-
                                    hearted,
Scatalogical verse, and bad puns, and once others get
                                    started
Just leave them alone. You should find, if they're
                                    playing their part,
That good conversation is sometimes a dying art.

3 - disposal

It's traditional to be self-indulgent and melodramatic
And send them up Nevis, or Scafell, or somewhere
                                    aquatic
Off a wild Cornish coast, sitting grim-faced and green
                                    in the stern

Of a mackerel-infested old tub, holding fast to the
                                                    urn.
But instead, put my elements into a battered old tin,
Label it "Commoner", then wander innocent in
To the British Museum, and seek out a comfortable
                                                  chair.
When you're suitably rested, go home. I'll just hang
                                        around there.

By the same author:

A Measured Response
novel - isbn 978-0-9926088-1-1

Teaching in FE
isbn 978-0-9926088-3-5

Managing Teachers in FE
isbn 978-0-9926088-4-2

For children

Quentin's Big Adventure
isbn 978-0-9926088-0-4

Reading and Thinking -
a Primary Reader
isbn 978-0-9926088-5-9

www.ingramcontent.com/pod-product-compliance
Lightning Source LLC
Chambersburg PA
CBHW061054050726
47592CB00004B/1676